Billy COOKS LIKE A MOTHER!

Billy COOKS LIKE A MOTHER!

A Guide to Starting Your Own Business
by Someone Who's Been There and Done That

Billy Kounoupis

Star City Publishing

Billy Cooks Like a Mother: A Guide to Starting Your Own Business by Someone Who's Been There and Done That
Copyright © 2012 by Billy Kounoupis
Published by Star City Publishing

For further information, contact the author at:
starcitypublishers@gmail.com
Star City Publishing
PO Box 1545
Bethlehem, PA 18016

www.billysdiner.com

Printed in the United States of America

Billy Cooks Like a Mother: A Guide to Starting Your Own Business by Someone Who's Been There and Done That
Billy Kounoupis

1. Author   2. Title   3. Business

Library of Congress Control Number: 2011940362

ISBN 13: 978-0-61555049-7

*To my mother Georgia Kounoupis. To my father,
Pete Kounoupis, and my brother, George Kounoupis,
whom I miss. They will live in my memory forever.
And to my beautiful and loving wife, Yanna, and my
wonderful children, Panayioti, Georgia, and Michael,
who bless my life with joy and happiness.*

JULY, 1957

TABLE OF CONTENTS

Preface

I can't believe I chose this life.

It's 4 a.m., Friday, September 29, 2000. It's my first day as a restaurant owner in over thirteen years, since my first miserable failure when I was twenty-one. This time things are going to be different. I'm no longer a little punk of twenty-one. I'm now thirty-five, with Yanna, my very pregnant wife, whom I adore.

We have settlement on our building today. My wife and I are nervous. We walk through the doors of what is to be our new place of business. Neither of us slept the night before. We open the doors and start to hear beeping. Holy crap! That's the alarm! I cannot for the life of me remember the code to turn it off. I begin running all around the place, trying to figure out where the light switches are. I find them, and I turn on the lights; thankfully, the alarm panel is near them. I grab some of the papers I'd been given, trying to find the alarm code. Meanwhile, the phone starts ringing. It's the alarm company, and they want me to recite the alarm code to them as well. The lady on the other end of the line is not sounding very sympathetic.

The sound of the alarm is so piercing that my wife and I think our eardrums will burst. Finally, I find the alarm code and key it in so the damn noise will stop. Just at that very moment the cops arrive. They pensively but authoritatively ask what we're doing there. My wife holds up a bottle of bleach and with her cute smile and a sarcastic tone says we are part of the cleaning crew. I introduce myself and my wife to the police officer as the new owners of Rudy's Newsstand. Unimpressed, the officer leaves.

My wife and I look at the clock. It's now 4:30, one and a half hours until opening. My wife starts focusing on getting the front of the house organized because we have no idea where anything is. We do not even have a system of how to serve or start filling orders in the kitchen. As she focuses on the front, I quickly inventory the kitchen to see what we have to start the day with. The former owners were kind enough to leave us some supplies to make it through. We just don't know if that's going to be enough. Upon review, we have fifty pounds of potatoes for home fries. I cook bacon and sausage and cut scrapple and grill it. I do as much preparation as possible, as much as one could do for the hoped-for big rush. I make fresh homemade soups and set up the line.

It's 5:45 a.m. My wife has the dining room ready and the coffee brewed. My heart starts pounding. At five minutes before six, a breath of fresh air walks through the door: Debbie, our waitress. She cleans the counter, grabs a cup of coffee, and lights a cigarette. I'm shocked. I ask myself, *Who smokes at 6 a.m.?* Debbie looks over at the two of us and asks, "Are you ready?" My wife and I look at each other, and with a strong but reluctant tone we answer, "You bet we are."

It's now 6:30, and not a single customer has walked in. I'm concerned. My wife and I put everything we had into this. My mom used her home as collateral to make this deal happen for us.

At last, at 6:45, a customer walks through the door. I'm ready to show off my culinary skills. We welcome him in unison, but all he asks is, "Do you have a bathroom?"

We're too entranced to give him a hard time, hoping against hope that when he comes out he will, maybe, order something, anything. A few moments go by. He comes out of the bathroom, walks past us, and proceeds to leave the premises. My wife turns to me and whispers loudly, "Who *does* that?" I, being Mr. Personality—or Mr. Doormat, in this case—thank the guy for using our restroom.

It is now 7 a.m. Another person walks through the door. It's Sebastian, our dishwasher, who does not speak a word of English. I can't complain, though. More work, less jabber. I take Sebastian back to the kitchen and speak loudly in part Greek and part English mixed with the very little Spanish I know. Ever notice how when people don't speak each other's language they try to make up for it by shouting? It's silly, and it doesn't work, but when you're stressed, you do what feels right. I'm impressed he has any clue at all as to what I'm trying to tell him. The whole day I attempt to communicate three things: "dish," "clean dish," and "scrubba scrubba mop," which is Billy-ese (the name I give to this hybrid of Greek, English, and Spanish) for "sweep the floor and mop."

At 7:10 a.m., a customer walks through the door with a big 7-Eleven cup into which he spits. A tobacco chewer. And I thought Debbie with the early morning smoking was bad! He orders a cup of coffee, which I assume he will drink since he already has a spittoon. He also orders two eggs scrambled with bacon. Oh happy day! I am border-line orgasmic, for it's our first real sale. I don't even mind that he's smoking a cigarette as he continues to spit in his cup. I begin to wonder if there are any other anatomical ways he can get tobacco into his system simultaneously.

It's now 7:45 a.m. Mr. Tobacco is gone, and we're $2.80 richer. Hurray! I can't help but laugh. Two dollars and eighty cents. *This* is why I went into business?

At 8 a.m., my mom, Georgia, walks through the door with a big smile. She makes the sign of the cross and offers a quick prayer, blessing us in our fledgling endeavor. She asks if she can put some change in our cash register. Yeah, like with our one, big, $2.80 sale we're going to run out of change! But instead I darn near break down and cry. The woman put her home up for collateral so I could open this place, and now she wants to fill the change drawer too.

I could continue to give you a minute-by-minute, blow-by-blow recap of my first day in business, but suf-fice it to say we built that $2.80 all the way up to…$115. Add to that about $200 in cigarettes, plus we sold a few newspapers and magazines, and that was our day. That pittance was for a full day's work for all of us—me, my wife, the waitress, the dishwasher, the people we owed, and all the overhead.

Was this going to work?

At the time, Rudy's Newsstand, the business we bought, was known as a place people came by to purchase lottery tickets, grab a basic and quick, cheap meal and maybe a cuppa Joe. This was not my vision of what I wanted. I wanted something different, a place with a cool, modern edge. I wanted to push the culinary envelope and do comfort food with flair.

After a little struggle with the concept change, gradually moving from being a newsstand that sold a little food to the kind of diner I'd always dreamed of running, my wife and my good friend George and I came up with the idea of ditching the Rudy's Newsstand name completely and branding ourselves as Billy's Downtown Diner. I mean, after a while I was also getting sick of being asked, "Which one of you is Rudy?" I also added the catchphrase "Not Your Ordinary Diner."

Now the real struggle started. Already broke, we had to redo the menus. My wife would experiment on an old PC, and our creative juices started to flow. That's when the screaming and shouting began between me and my wife. Not because we didn't love and respect one another, but because of our creative differences. We would create crazy dishes like the Mexican Omelette, Berry Crunch Toast, the Cabo Wabo Omelette, the Copacabana Omelette, and Tonga Toast. Trust me, the ingredients to these and our other brainstorms were unique and not found anywhere in the Lehigh Valley, where we are, about sixty miles north of Philadelphia. We would fight over ingredients, prices, even the names of dishes. My wife challenged me on everything. It was annoying, but I know why she did it. She wanted us to be 100 percent certain of what our menus should be. I mean, if you don't have someone to argue with, how will you ever know you're right (or wrong)?

After years of hard work and struggles—financially, emotionally, and physically—we struck pay dirt in 2005 when we won our first award, *Lehigh Valley* magazine's Best Breakfast in the Lehigh Valley. We were utterly in awe. We couldn't believe we had won an award. Thousands of people voted our place number one. It was something we never took for granted and something we never expected. Who expects a little sixty-five-seat diner that has been in business for only four years to compete with the restaurant giants of the Lehigh Valley that have been around for twenty-five or in some cases fifty years?

Then something funny happened. Other Lehigh Valley magazines gave us Best Diner in 2007, 2008, and

2009 and Best Breakfast in 2006, 2007, 2008, 2009, and 2010 as well as two Decadent Dish awards.

I look back at this, and it's still too surreal for me. We went from serving a few hundred people a week to serving close to 5,000 people every single week. We went from selling a few pounds of home fries a week to over 1,000 pounds per week. We went from 720 or so eggs to almost 5,000 eggs per week. My wife and I are still active in our diner, and we always try to be the most original at what we do. We were the first diner in the history of the Lehigh Valley to go smoke-free—which may have cost us that first customer of ours, the one who chewed and smoked at the same time, but we didn't care. We preferred it that way, and so did our most loyal customers. This was in 2001, six years before smoke-free became mandatory. We started burning our own CDs so we could control the audio ambiance, added plasma screen TVs, used surround-sound, sold merchandise, but most important, for as much as we added to the place's atmosphere, we never forgot the first and most-crucial ingredient, serving our customers. It was our obligation and our honor to give them the very best of everything we could; they deserved nothing less.

It is now 2011. I still wake up at 6 a.m. and leave the restaurant around 4:30 p.m. seven days a week. I can honestly say I love what I do, and serving our customers is something I will never take for granted. All I can say is thank you Bethlehem and the Lehigh Valley for letting us be a part of your life and you being a part of ours. I love you, and I look forward to serving you in our little diner in Bethlehem to my last day on earth.

Acknowledgments

The City of Bethlehem, the Lehigh Valley, and all of our loyal customers who were with us from the beginning.

The crew of Billy's Downtown Diner: you're the best!

My wife, Yanna: without you there would have been no Billy's Downtown Diner.

My mom, Georgia Kounoupis, the greatest mom in the world: there would have been no second chance for me without you.

My children, Panayioti, Georgia, and Michael: you three fill my heart with happiness, joy, and love.

My father-in-law, Michael: you are not only a great donut maker but an awesome DAD.

Uncle Gus, Thea Eleni, Thea Dora, Theo Panayioti, Theo Yanni, Thea Irene, Thea Dimitra, Thea Penelope, and Thea Eleni of Greece: I LOVE YOU!

Dean Tantaros, a great brother and my best friend, la la la.

John Freund, Esquire, my martini buddy.

Keith Bachman, CPA, my great friend and numbers guy.

 Christopher Werley. The ultimate luxury and lifestyle publisher as well as my good friend, (valleysocialmag.com).

Larry Holmes, Jr.: we need a Vegas trip, bro!

John Callahan, mayor of Bethlehem: thanks for your support and friendship.

My cousins, Johnny Zannakis, Spiro Kounoupis, George C. Kounoupis, and Maria Manakos: xoxo always.

To all of our koumbari and godchildren: thank you for allowing us to be part of your family and for being a part of ours. I love you.

Peter "the eye" Gourniak, the photographer that shot me (petergourniak.com).

Tim Miller Photography (timmillerphoto.com); thank you for the great photos. You are truly a great artist.

Introduction

I have been asked many times, why write a book about business? What are your qualifications? I'm not a chef or a college graduate. Hell, I barely graduated high school. There were 600 students in my graduating class, and I was ranked 599! I looked over at 600 and said, "Dude, you're an idiot!" Just kidding. But the fact is I didn't graduate at the top of my class, not by a long shot. Not only that, but I also *felt* like I was at the bottom of the barrel.

I think what actually drove me to succeed was my hero, my father, Pete Kounoupis. I lost my dad before I graduated high school due to a doctor's misdiagnosis.

Let me share with you the event that completely changed my life forever. When I was fifteen, I walked to my parents' diner after school, a daily event since my mom, Georgia, and my father, Pete, were workaholics. To my surprise that day, my mom and dad were not in the diner. I knew something was up, but I couldn't put my finger on it till the phone rang. I answered; it was the hospital asking me to come. I went to the kitchen and told Paul, the cook, "I need your car." He said, "No way! You don't have a license." I told him the hospital had called and my dad was sick. He reluctantly gave me his keys, and I drove to the hospital. When I arrived, I saw my family in tears. They said my dad was not going to make it.

I went into my dad's room, and I couldn't control my sobbing. My dad said with a smile, "Why're you crying?" I told him I was scared and couldn't live without him. He said, "Don't be scared of anything. Death is a part of life, and life is not a dress rehearsal." He said, "Realize that you live in a country of endless opportunities, and you have so many more opportunities than I did."

At the time I had no clue what he was talking about, but I get it now that I am older and wiser. My dad left his homeland of Sparta, Greece, during World War II, with no education, on a ship bound for America. Heck, he couldn't even speak the language. He came though Ellis Island, spent the night in a bus terminal, found a job, married the love of his life, and in ten years opened his first restaurant, and then his second, and then a night-club. How did he pull it off? Very simple: hard work, smart work, a vision, and a no-excuse attitude. And my mother shared his vision and worked just as hard.

My dad was so right. I had 100 times more opportunity to succeed than he ever had. First, I was born and raised in the best country in the world, the United States of America, a country that embraces entrepreneurship. My father had left the old country with twenty bucks in his pocket. I had everything, and he had had nothing.

Actually, that's not true. He had an entrepreneurial spirit, the ambition and desire to stake his claim in the world and succeed. He knew you couldn't get rich in this world working for someone else; you needed to do your own thing and have something to call your own. Here, in America, he knew he could grab hold of that and make it happen.

Today, more than ever, working for and being beholden to the folks in corporate America is an exercise in self-hatred. They don't care about you. They will take from you everything you're willing to give them and then spit you out and replace you with a twelve-year-old from a third world country who will work for a pack of Lucky Strikes. Working for The Man means you have zero control over your own destiny.

The only antidote to this reality is entrepreneurialism. Working for myself, I could still fail, but it would be *my own* failure, not some other guy's. We live in a country with more millionaires than any other, but only a handful of them got there by working for someone else. All the rest got there by staking their own claim and doing their own thing.

What was I waiting for? What are *you* waiting for?

1

So You Want to Start Your Own Business

Congratulations! You're making a great choice and a big step toward being free from The Man and instead *being* The Man. Your journey is going to be like the movie *300*. It will be you against many, but trust me, next to being a proud parent, making your business dreams come true is probably the most awesome thing you will do, so let's begin this journey.

First, you must determine the type of business you want. Be honest with yourself and take a basic self-evaluation test. Ask yourself these questions:

1. What am I good at and why?
2. What is my idea?
3. Can I visualize my future business?
4. Is there a market for what I want to do?
5. Do I love what I want to do? (Trust me—the money will come if you are passionate about what you do. If you are doing it just for the money, chances are you will fail.)
6. What is my concept?

As we go forward in this book and continue to ask these questions, I will share with you how I answered them for myself and why, because as basic as these questions are, you need to be thorough in order to determine your self-worth.

Here are my answers, in order:

1. Sales, marketing, and cooking.
2. Casual cuisine with a flair, reasonably priced, fresh, delivered with super-fast service.
3. When I closed my eyes, I saw my wall filled with photos of people I had met who have inspired my life and brought

me funny memories. I saw plasma TVs and a surround-sound system playing cool music that touched my soul, comfortable booths, an open-concept kitchen, big plates filled with mounds of cool dishes my wife, Yanna, and I created, a menu that was innovative and presented items not ordinarily served with breakfast, and menu covers embracing our beautiful city of Bethlehem.

4. We did some basic research to check what some of the most popular foods in our country were. We also looked into casual dining places, the most popular eateries on the East Coast as well as the West Coast. This told us the basic types of meals folks liked. But after doing so, we took what we'd learned and pretty much did our own thing. Our concept was to play with our food, something kids all over the world are told not to do…unless they want to someday become a chef.

In other words, we knew we had no

patent on omelettes, nor did anyone else, but we knew people liked them. From there we added our own not-so-ordinary twists. For example, I happen to like sun-dried tomatoes better than regular ones. Was there a market for that? I thought so, and I was willing to put my money where my mouth was. I knew I couldn't and wouldn't just copy what other people were doing even if they were wildly successful. I mean, if I did that, why wouldn't my customers just go to the original place? I'd rather people copied me!

5. Yes, yes, and yes. I have spent over half my life in the restaurant business. If I wasn't in a kitchen preparing food, I worked for a company that sold food. I have never dabbled in anything else but the restaurant industry, which, I suppose, means I have simply never been a dabbler period.

6. As I saw it, I had four main choices to choose from: First, there was *fast food*. I decided against that because

those types of places have minimal seating, minimal service, and one of the toughest concepts in which to succeed. Because of the low price point of their products, chains really dominate that market.

Option two was *ethnic cuisine*. Because this is so specialized, it can really narrow your demographic group. For instance, if you want a burger, you don't go to a Chinese restaurant.

Option three was *fine dining*. This style of cuisine was definitely not for me for many reasons: it requires impeccable, almost obsessive attention to detail; it is very labor intensive; and it is a niche market that is great for special occasions but not for everyday dining and customer loyalty.

Option four was *casual*. Yeah baby, that was how I wanted to roll. This was the style of cuisine I chose because it bridges the gap between fast food and full service and because it's moderately priced, it enables me to turn tables

around rapidly, and overall it is probably the most successful style of eating
establishment.

Once you have decided on your
direction or concept, embrace it and
believe in it. Remember, if you don't
love what you do, chances are nobody
else will either.

2

Serious Business

Business is war—a truthful statement, but what does it really mean? To most people it means watching out for the competition, being ever-mindful of theft, and in general watching your back. Well, all those definitions apply, but to me there is another key definition: the internal struggle you must have with yourself.

Let me give you an example: You are employed at the XYZ Corporation. It is not important whether it's a multinational conglomerate or a small diner. It's the place to which you have given your blood, sweat, and tears for years. Everyone admires your work ethic and notices your loyalty and all your great talents, your passion, and your common sense. Of course, humble and overworked you don't notice your own self-worth. Then on that one defining day at work something snaps, and you realize you're burning out. You begin doing just the minimum amount of work to keep your job, and your boss pays you just enough to keep you around. You realize a work-related divorce is imminent. What do you do? Should you stay and be miserable, or should you go for the American Dream of being your own boss and controlling your own destiny?

The key issue is security. When I worked as a restaurant cook, dishwasher, and manager, I was also working for corporate America, and what I noticed is that job security in corporate America is tenuous at best. It's all about merger after merger, profits, profits, profits, and trim, trim, trim that fat. I had never experienced such stress levels, not even when I was broke and struggling in my own business. Owner-operated businesses were sometimes even worse. My bosses, the owners of the businesses, seemed almost bipolar—inconsistent and mean-tempered and very hard to work for. But what the hell, I needed the job.

At that point I realized what a risk I was taking *working for others*! It was this realization that the biggest risk is in doing something you don't like and doing it every day for other people, those who completely control your life and your livelihood and who, when the going got tough, would kick you off the last life raft just to save themselves. Heck, working for someone else is so shaky you could get the boot simply because your boss had a fight with his wife that day or because he didn't like the way you parted your hair. I got ticked off that I found this out later rather than sooner.

After I realized this, I had to convince myself, my family, and my peers I could do something else—be my own boss. Let me put it like this: this was not my first shot in business. I had been in it before, and wow, what a disaster! But even knowing the headaches, I knew in my heart and soul that to follow any other path would just make me more and more miserable and that instead of having greater security in life I would have only less.

"Serious business" is the internal struggle you have to have with yourself. What is your threshold for pain? What are you willing to do? Are you willing to leverage your home, your life, and your friends? Are you prepared to give it your all and live your life with no excuses? Are you prepared to give your customers what they want? Are you willing to sideline your ego and seek advice from others? If you are, welcome to the most elite club. You are part of the *Yes I Can and Will* club! This is the club that made America great. This is why people fled their native lands and came here, leaving their families and homes for the great unknown. Think about it. Most of them never went back. I can mention numerous Greeks in my family who never went back. Ask any of them if the journey was worth it. Ask any Asian, Italian, Greek, or any other immigrant. All these people were tough, and they refused to be lulled into complacency, which is what I consider a major cause of cancer in business, right next to stupidity. Remember, always seek good advice and understand the consequences of your decisions.

If you are chanting to yourself, "Billy is right," then you must do two things: pray to God for support, and take a good look at yourself in the mirror. Take a moment and a deep breath, and when you're ready, say to yourself, "I will be my own boss. I am no better than anyone else, and no one is better than me." Then start planning your success. If you are not ready for this, put the book down now. *Do not read any further*. If you can't make a commitment to yourself, you are not ready for big things.

3

Competitive Analysis—Choosing a Concept

When choosing a concept for your future business, you need to know your market. Don't misunderstand me; you must believe in your concept and understand it, and it is very important for you to execute it properly. Let me simplify why this section is so important. Let's assume I know and understand what my business needs, and I totally believe in it. If I don't *execute properly*, I'm screwed.

Imagine walking into the most beautiful restaurant, cosmetically speaking. You sit in beautiful, plush chairs. Your waiter greets you and asks what you would like to order. You are so excited being at this place and you are hungry, so you place your order. You decide you want the house salad without the walnuts because you have allergies, and the filet mignon, medium rare, and a nice cool beer to accompany your meal. You wait and wait for your meal. First the salad comes out. The lettuce is wilted, and there *are* walnuts, and then a few minutes later your steak comes out overcooked, and the cool beer you ordered is a glass of wine. Obviously, you would be pissed and justifiably so. Regardless of how beautiful this restaurant is, none of that matters because your order and the service sucked. Remember, aesthetics are important, but execution is where the substance is.

In business, it is important to follow your instincts, but do not be foolish. *Do your demographic surveys.* There are plenty of Websites, including fedstat.com and demographics.com, that can provide you with this information.

Knowledge is power. Some may argue that opening a high-end luxury business is a bad idea in a lower-income area, but sometimes it works. You might find yourself successful because you have no competition! On the other hand you might go broke. The most important thing is to be purposeful. *Know* what you're getting into. Also, have a fallback position. If your high-end venture is failing, prepare to either go more low-end or else prepare to move the whole concept to where the demographics favor you more. But think this through in advance; don't let everything be an accident, good or bad!

Competition has always existed and always will exist. Get used to it. Thirty years ago, competition was not as tough as it is today, when there are specialty shops for nearly everything. Worse than that, there are tons of nationwide chains that keep adding more and more goods and services. Even gas stations and convenience stores now serve hot fast food, a concern for people in the restaurant business such as me. They're not really diners, but if you're in a hurry, they can replace a customer's need for one.

Whatever it is you do, there are probably similar operations. Is it fair? No. But then again life isn't fair, so you'd better get used to it. In Manhattan, over 800 restaurants close every year. Yes, I said close; not open, but close. Ouch!

Know what you are getting into. *Know your competition.* All this is important because without proper research you might not know how to price your services or your menu. Remember, a fair price is what consumers are willing to pay, and that is why it's important for you to research to determine what is fair and reasonable.

There are many theories and much controversy about competition, but the one thing everyone agrees on is that it is better to know what you are doing and blunder than to blunder because *you had no idea what was going on*!

I'll give you an example of this. People argue about whether flooding a geographic area with a certain kind of business is smart or not. Perfect example: Go to New York City and look for the diamond district. There's an entire block or two of nothing but jewelers, jewelers, jewelers. In a way it makes no sense at all. People could comparison shop you all day long. That's the bad part. The good part is that all those looking for engagement rings in New York know to go to this part of town and they'll have a million choices. Again, we can argue forever whether this is good or bad for the merchants, but it is what it is. More important, all the jewelers there know the score. Being next to their competition is something they knew about going in.

What's universally *dumb*, on the other hand, is opening up a jewelry store and having no idea there's a big jewelry chain two blocks away, or else discovering far too late that another jeweler is planning on opening up right next door to you six months after you've just opened your doors. A good businessperson would *know* where the competition was and would *know* what was going on in the neighborhood. Good businesspeople have an ear to the ground at all times. They speak to the other local businesses and landlords. They join the chamber of commerce or the local merchants' association if for no other reason than to pick up on all the gossip—and I don't mean finding out who drinks too much or who runs around on his wife. Know the comings and goings in your area. Know what competitors are coming in, both big and small (but especially big).

Shop your competition. If you're a dentist, send your sister-in-law to that new guy in town to get her teeth cleaned. Ask her to note the prices, what the place looks like inside, whether they overtly push any particular optional services, etc. In other words, do reconnaissance. Only then can you truly know what you're up against, and you won't be caught off-guard. Maybe the other dentist has some great concept you could add to your own mix, or maybe you'll see the flaws and the follies to his or her approach. If you're asked about why you're not doing the same thing, you'll have an answer already prepared. But most of all, *know what you competition is charging*! You can't have a proper handle on your price niche if you don't even know what's going on outside your door. For example, you may *think* you're a low-end, bargain guy because you sell stuff regarded as commonplace and not fancy (in food, think hotdogs or cheeseburgers). You may also have a very plain, down-homey atmosphere. But your prices may be outrageous! How would you know if you didn't shop around? I'm in the Lehigh Valley. I can't charge New York prices. I'd like to, but the market won't sustain it. I'm sure if I were in New York, my prices would be considered dirt cheap—*too* cheap. I'd be leaving money on the table, so to speak, and that's not smart business.

Will this knowledge cause you to make changes? Possibly. If a competitor moves in right next to you, you don't necessarily have to move, but the sooner you know about it, the sooner you can make plans to compete and thrive. Don't get caught with your pants around your ankles. Know what's going on, and analyze how to compete and win!

4

Doing the Deal

My father, God rest his soul, said to me, "Business is like sports. You need a team of people in order to succeed, and to succeed in business you need three things: a great lawyer, a great CPA, and a great doctor." I will elaborate on all three later on, but I will say this again: you need a team of pros to protect your ass…ets. Yeah, assets—that's what I meant. Know your limitations. Just because you're a great mechanic or chef does not mean you're a great lawyer or CPA, and, well, medicine… You get the idea.

Okay, let's get into the heart of the matter. In business,

the reason you need a team is to keep your emotions out of your deal. As you become a seasoned pro in business, this will get easier, but first-timers in business, please read this carefully.

Your success in business is highly dependent on the deals you make at the beginning. Let's assume you want to open a sandwich spot. You have two great choices for a location. One is $1,200 per month while the other is $3,800. Choose the second one and you'll have $1,600 less in profits. *But...*the *price* of something and the *value* of something are two completely different things. The $1,200-a-month place might be a craphole worth only about $600 per month, while the $3,800 place might be very energy efficient and have loads of off-street parking and is actually undervalued by around $1,000 per month. Who knows? Answer: *You* must know! You must research this stuff before signing that lease.

Unfortunately, those are only the basics; it does not stop here. In a lease, there is the fine print and terms like *triple net lease*. No matter how you slice and dice it, legalese is a very complicated language. Stick to what you know, and let the pros handle the rest. If you don't, you'll be swimming in dangerous waters, and it might be too late for a lawyer to save you later on. Never be penny-wise and pound-foolish in business.

As you do deals, you will come to terms with the emotional side of things, for instance, buyer's remorse and seller's remorse. Your emotions can run wild when you're doing a deal; in order to survive you have to push your emotions aside and concentrate on the numbers and the logic.

Also, don't be afraid to trust your gut. If you find yourself sitting across from some guy who gives you a bad feeling, you're probably right. This is a case in which instincts are right more often than wrong. Never feel you absolutely have to take a particular deal or do a deal with one particular person. I know that at the time you might be tempted to feel that way, but let it pass. Even animals in the forest know how to smell danger. It's something God gave us all. Don't push aside the gift.

You also have to live within your means. Maybe you will come to realize you simply do not have enough funding to begin your business right now. If it's going to take $80,000 to get your business off the ground successfully and you have only $40,000, it's better to do it right for $80,000 than to blow your $40,000 when you know you're going to fail. Better to wait and get more money together than to shoot your entire fortune on a losing venture.

Doing deals is like playing poker. The top pros might

do a bluff now and then to keep the other players honest, but the best players know when it's time to push all their chips into the middle of the table. They have discipline and self-control. They know the odds. They watch how the cards fall, and they study their opponents. They don't just get drunk and say, "Oh, what the hell." If they did, they would never be on TV making big bucks in tournaments. All those same things hold true with doing business deals. Think like a poker pro. If you don't have the cards this hand, toss those rags aside and wait for the next hand. Go all-in only on a winner; don't back a loser.

They say you can learn more from failure than success. If that's true, I must be a genius, for I have failed, yessiree. I've changed some of the details to protect the incompetent (in most of the story that would be me), but here's a classic story of how one falls into a bad deal:

I had a shot at opening a second location. It was something I really wanted to do; I just needed the right place. Well, the right place popped up, or so it seemed. It had parking (what you hear behind you is angels singing). A real, honest-to-goodness, private parking lot in a downtown. This is like finding gold in a box of Lucky Charms. I had to have it. The price was steep, but I lined up my financing, and I was ready to pounce fast because I anticipated a bidding war. It needed renovations, which was not surprising. Most every place you take over needs renovations. The problem was, once I brought contractors and building inspectors in and they looked around, the renovation costs jumped by 500 percent. Sheesh! I'm sorry, but nobody budgets for 500 percent increases.

What happened was I had put a certain amount of money down as a good faith deposit in order to even get to this particular point in the deal. I could get it back if I asked for it right away, but after a certain number of days the money became the possession of the seller.

I waited too long. I was indecisive. It was like the guy who smells gas, waits a minute, and then screams "Run!" except by the time he gets to "R—" the building has already exploded. That was me. I wanted that deal so darn badly that even with the astronomical renovation costs I was still mulling it over, trying to line up the additional financing.

Ego. I was so full of myself that I figured I could make the deal work even at this highly, highly, highly inflated price. Dumb, dumb, dumb. The numbers would have never worked. I would have had to have customers lined up down the block all day long for years in order to make a profit. But the ego doesn't think like that. It says, "You're Billy! You can do this!" By the time sanity returned and booted ego to the curb, it was a choice of either walking away from a six-figure deposit or taking on a load of debt I might never get out from under.

I punted. I left six figures on the table and went home humiliated. It's one thing to invest in yourself, fight hard, and lose; it's another thing entirely to lose money simply for the opportunity to *look* at a deal, but in the end that's just what I had done. Bottom line: I should have grabbed my deposit back when I had the chance. Bad deal. I blew it.

5

Choosing a Lawyer

If you're doing business, hire a business lawyer, not a criminal lawyer. Most lawyers have a specialty such as malpractice or employment. Beware the jack-of-all-trades lawyers. That's like going to a podiatrist for a heart operation.

The basics of hiring a lawyer

Interview lawyers. Ask them what type of law they practice, how long they have practiced, and if they are licensed in your state. Ask them about the last deals they did, specify what you need done, and ask what their costs are to do your deal. A lot of lawyers will claim nondisclosure when you ask them the names of their clients, but ask them simply for references; they might have the permission of certain clients willing to vouch for them. Of course, be aware that these will always be people who think the world of them. In certain settings it is often easier to simply ask around and find out whom your friends or people you respect use or if they have heard of the person you're considering. A lawyer who is a good person, good at what he or she does, will have good word of mouth on the street.

Remember, a business lawyer can help you from the planning stage of your business by evaluating the potential liabilities and guide you on how to protect yourself whether by forming an LLC, a corporation, a partnership, etc. Also remember that people are sue-happy. These days we have age discrimination, sexual harassment, you name it. I speak from experience. Hire a lawyer. Protect yourself, your family, and your business.

A good business lawyer is almost a complete business advisor. Most small-business people don't have access to a person who does just that—consulting and business advising. The closest and most affordable thing you may have is that lawyer of yours. Pick his or her brain.

It's good to use one with lots of local ties. They know the bankers, they know the accountants, they know the landlords, and they know the towns. They're the people who can say, "You don't want to open in that town. The local zoning and planning boards will just abuse you and make you spend millions just to put up a sign and change the usage. Instead, go to the next town down the road. They're more sensible and business-friendly." Lawyers know this because they have to make presentations before those boards all the time.

Good business lawyers can grease the wheels for you with banks. Some will call their bankers on your behalf—maybe they play golf together—and make an introduction for you. Lawyers are some of the most powerful people on your team, so don't be afraid to use them. This also underscores why it's important to hire the right one. If you hire the lawyer everyone in town hates or thinks is a clown, you're in for trouble. Check them out thoroughly.

Lawyers must also be responsive to your needs. Some are real ivory-tower guys who have such big practices they cannot keep track of all their deals. While it may be good to have someone with a large practice—which usually indicates significant success—the bigger the guy is, the slower he may move. If you're trying to buy a business and there are numerous other suitors, you don't want a lawyer who takes a week or two to return your calls. That can kill your deal because your potential partner in the deal will instead go with the buyer who can move more quickly.

6

CPA or Accountant

I know the question: what's the big freakin' difference between an accountant and a CPA? For starters, a CPA has a degree in accounting and has to pass an exam—harder than the legal bar, I hear—to become licensed in the state in which they want to practice. CPAs are held to a pretty high standard; they follow a strict ethical code and must continually reeducate themselves to keep up with new industry rules and regulations.

An accountant is basically someone who's good at math.

Personally I vote the CPA ticket.

Now why do you need a numbers guy in the first place? Because it is one of the most crucial necessities in business. You cannot work eighteen-hour shifts building your business and also handle payroll, taxes, and all that other related stuff. But remember, no matter how great your CPA is, *sign your own checks*!

A CPA will have a positive effect on your business by helping you put accounting systems in place, organizing your payroll, analyzing your financial information, and so on. Knowing and understanding your financial liabilities is key to your success. And remember, in business, Uncle Sam is your partner too, and he wants his money no matter what; if you do not have a loving, respectful relationship with him and obey his laws, say bye-bye to your business, house, and everything else you have, including your credit. And once he is done with that, there is potential jail time.

Let's talk a minute about analyzing your payroll and your financial information. Your CPA is like a second set of eyes, and a neutral one at that. You, you're working your business every day of the week, so after a while you can begin to lose perspective. You see something you want for your business, and you want to go right out and buy it. You justify it in your mind, and that's that. As immersed as you are in your business and loving it as you do, you're not always the best judge of whether you can truly afford something.

Enter the CPA, the person to turn to when you feel you should be making more money than you are. After looking at your books, he or she might be easily able to say, "Wow, you sure spent a lot on equipment last year. Do you really need all this stuff?" Your CPA won't personally care one way or the other, but a question like that should be a wake-up call.

Even better than a wake-up call is a *preventative* wake-up call. Instead of waiting until you've already put yourself in debt, stop by your CPA's office and ask whether you can afford that new gadget, or spend more money on advertising, or what have you. He or she will have no personal stake in what you do, so you'll get just the facts, which is what you need.

The other big things your CPA can give you guidance with is payroll and labor. These are your most controllable costs. Again, I know, you start work, work, working your business and you think, *I need another person* and then not long after, *Oh, now I need another person.* You don't want someone who is doing good work for you to leave, so you say to yourself, "I'll give her a raise. That'll keep her happy." Yeah, but will *you* be happy when that raise comes out of *your* pocket? Can you afford it? Again, before you go on the hook for it, ask your CPA.

Business is serious. Know what you are getting into, and hire the best. As always, make sure your CPA is licensed where you do business.

7

Somebody Get Me a Doctor!

Being your own boss has many perks. The downside is you will have high stress levels. Health is paramount in life and in business. You will experience high stress levels regardless of how successful you are, and if you're not successful, the levels of stress can be even worse. Modern science tells us that stress is a strain on all of our physical systems. And if your body doesn't work, you don't work; if you don't work, you don't make money.

Schedule your annual checkups. Don't go to doctors just when you're feeling ill. You gotta maintain your car, don't you? What's more important, you or your Toyota?

If you think you're getting sick, go to your doctor. *Have* a doctor. Don't be one of those dummies who go to the emergency room whenever something happens to them. That costs a bundle, and there's no continuity of care.

Let me make one blanket statement about lawyers, CPAs, and doctors: better to have them and not need them than to need them and not have them.

While we're on the topic of health, let me talk a little here about mental health. Owning your own business takes a toll on you, and don't believe anyone who tells you otherwise. I know that a lot of people who work for others think, *Yeah, I'm gonna open my own place, and it's gonna be Easy Street.* Baloney!

Listen, I know it's tough working for someone else. Mudslides roll downhill. But here's where people with what we call an "employee mentality" get it all wrong. As an employee, you know those big headaches, the ones where you have to go get the boss? When you *are* the boss, those are all yours, and yes, they're the biggest headaches of all.

Hours? Most employees work nine to five. Owners? They work until the job is done, and if that means all night long, it's all night long.

How is this on your mental health? Not so good

sometimes. The employee knows what he or she is going to earn each week in most occupations. Owners? Feast or famine. If things are going badly, everyone and everything gets paid except you. That's stressful.

Being the owner puts a lot more pressure on a marriage and on a family. Yes, I have a unique situation since I've incorporated my family into my business, but most other guys have work widows—wives who see them as often as military spouses see their husbands or wives who are deployed in Iraq. I've seen business ownership cost a lot of people their marriages. And even when husband and wife work together, there are strains. Some couples can't pull it off successfully. They need a break from each other once in a while or else they go crazy.

Just as I'm not afraid to go to a regular medical doctor, if you're experiencing problems in your marriage or you're just not feeling right emotionally, don't be afraid to admit it to a professional. Sometimes it takes a skilled neutral observer to give you the key to unlocking what's ailing you. No business, no amount of money is worth your health or your family. When people talk about having it all, it means a well-rounded life, not just a pile of money and no one to share it with.

The overwork that often accompanies owning your own business can also lead to very unhealthy lifestyle choices. I work around food all day long. Think that doesn't make me want to eat? Of course it does! There are all kinds of unhealthy eating: nervous eating, depressive eating, I-don't-want-to-waste-food-so-I'll-eat-it-myself eating. Then there are the people who get out of work after an eighteen-hour day and say, "I need a drink." Need I say more? Lots of alcoholic business owners out there. Exercise? A person who has a perfectly regular schedule can say, "I work nine to five. I'll get up each day a little early, go to the gym, and then be at work right on time." That's wonderful! But the owner? I'll bet that with their crazy hours, more business owners have gym memberships they never use than any other class of people. Gyms should market to us like crazy, knowing they'll be getting our money and never have to give us anything in return!

Eat well. Get some exercise. Clear your head in a healthy way. Don't drink too much. We all know these things to be true, but when you own your own business, not only are they harder to do, they're even more imperative. But do them. Do it for yourself, and do it for your loved ones. They don't just want your money, they want *you*!

8

Location, Location, Location!

We always hear people say the most important thing in business is location. That's true, and as a businessman I urge you not to take location for granted. Let me elaborate before we actually talk about why location is important.

First, I've seen many businesses fail in great locations, and I've seen many businesses thrive in so-so locations. Why do you think that happens? Because of execution, getting the proper deal, and working through emotions.

Very few businesses fail for one specific reason. There are usually multiple reasons, such as the owner is a quitter, has no understanding of business, or in some cases has more money than brains (I've never seen anyone have too much brains). In my restaurant, I have always said there are two types of recipes: a recipe for success and a recipe for disaster. The willingness to succeed is in you. Now that I got that off my chest, let's talk about location.

What makes a great location? A lot of big things plus common sense, such as considering *traffic flow*. I don't know many successful businesses on remote country roads. You have to be where the cars and the foot traffic are plentiful.

I am certain you know the difference between a desert and a highway: *visibility*. You can have great traffic flow, but you have to be noticed. That's why most franchises and offices get the *corner spots*. You might think you'll do well because you're on a busy thoroughfare, but your spot may be squashed up against some other place, and your signage might not peek through.

I can't stress *parking* and *accessibility* enough. If your building holds 200 people but there's parking for only two cars, you've got a real challenge. At Billy's, we have only on-street parking, no parking lot. This doesn't make our life easy. Then again, consider all the people with restaurants in Manhattan. There's hardly any on-street parking at all, and garages cost more than your meal! How do they make it? They make it because people are attracted to Manhattan and they gotta eat, so they deal with the inconvenience. In a perfect world, the business owner would offer no inconvenience to his or her customers, but we rarely have such perfect situations.

Because of the reputation we've built up, people line up in the rain down the street in order to eat at Billy's. I truly wish I could make our customers' lives easier with private off-street parking, but at our location that's simply not to be. Were I starting from scratch, that's an amenity I would look for, no doubt about it. But when I started Billy's, it was in a location I could afford, and so I took it. A place with a parking lot would have cost more than I could have afforded at the time. These are the trade-offs you must face as an entrepreneur. Part of why we've made it, in addition to how good we are, is that we have a nice flow of trade from local colleges, offices, and residences, we have walk-ins and drive-bys, and our city is a destination location. We may not be Manhattan, but we like to think we've got a miniature version of Manhattan amenities, i.e., we're not out in the middle of nowhere.

You also don't want to be on a highway with a divider that forces people coming from one direction to have to drive a mile past you and then turn around in order to come into your parking lot. People are lazy. They'll just come to visit you on the days when they're coming from the other direction or not at all.

Be handicap accessible, too. It's not just for handicapped people; those ramps and elevators are good for the elderly as well. Remember, substance in what you do is very important, but so is convenience.

Also, make sure you research present and future *traffic patterns*. Check with the highway department or local agencies to see if they are planning any major roadwork that might disrupt accessibility to your business. Imagine opening up a new business—the most crucial time in your business' life cycle—and a major detour will be taking people away from or around your location for the next nine months.

Then there is the *size* of your site, which is very important because it needs to be big enough to handle your business. Of course, some people pick a site way too big for the amount of business they will do. In that case they're paying for tons of wasted space, which can kill a business. Every square foot of business space has to pay for itself.

I mentioned the importance of the deal. Can you afford your location? *Affordability* is also key. I can find you some great commercial space, but if it costs you too much, you'll probably be broke by the end of your first week. The perfect location is the spot that has all the good amenities and also makes financial sense.

Don't overlook the *condition* of the site. Are there code violations? What kind of shape is it in?

In my opinion, the last thing of major importance in choosing a location for your business is *crime*. As important as everything else I mentioned is, this may be the most important. People need to feel safe. No matter how great your product is, if your customers have to risk their lives to get it, then it's not worth it.

9

Design

When you're developing your business, design is paramount. You really need to give it thought, because your design will affect your bottom line. Also, depending on your business, there might be privacy issues. I realize this is basic, but it's very important. Let me give you a few different examples of effects and costs of three different types of businesses.

First, a mortgage company. You need at least a waiting room, a conference room, and an office. Second, a doctor's office. You'll need at least a waiting room and patient rooms designed for privacy. Third is a restaurant or bar.

For these, the design serves a few different purposes. If you are developing a nightclub, chances are you want to direct customers to the bar. If a restaurant, you need easy access to tables, for waitstaff to attend to guests, and for comfort—diners don't like other tables too close to them. The key element is simplicity. You always want the wow factor, but don't go overboard.

No business has made more of a science out of space design than have casinos. They always make sure they are secretly controlling your every move. Their entire shtick is to keep you moving toward places where you will spend the most money, such as the casino floor itself. They want you to eat, but they don't make big money on that. They want you to drink, but in most cases they give that away for free. They want you to see shows, but that's not a super-big money maker for them either. In the end, they want you to *gamble*. And when it comes to gambling, they want to take away every penny you walked in with. That means they want you to be enticed to gamble no matter which direction you turn, and they want you to spend a lot when you do it. With slot machines, they make sure they put the prettiest and most expensive ones right near the entrances so you can't miss them. They stick the cheap little old machines in the back. They want you to have to walk past much-more exciting things before you hit those crappy old nickel slots.

Your business must think along these same lines. Restaurants usually have tables by the windows so they can seat people there first and make the place look busy from the outside. Nobody likes to go to an empty restaurant. Why is it empty? Do they have mice?

Your design must allow for a good, efficient flow that directs your customers to do what it is you want them to do. It must also allow your help to do what you want *them* to do.

Most businesses usually remodel every two years with a new paint job or paintings or furniture. Cleanliness and organization are key ingredients. And don't forget, no matter how nice your space is, you still need to execute what you are doing. How many times have you walked into a restaurant that looked great but the food was terrible? How many times have you walked into a place that was clean with no frills but the food kicked ass? Where would you prefer to spend your hard-earned money?

Here are some back-to-the-basics considerations we gave to our designer for Billy's Downtown Diner: entrance, music, art, hostess station, cashier station, and small seating area. We of course knew the most expensive part of the restaurant was the kitchen. We needed it to be as efficient as possible and not take up too much space. Customers pay to sit in the dining room, not in the kitchen. The bigger the kitchen, the smaller the dining area.

In my business, the office is the least important. Mine is the size of a broom closet. I use it only to count cash drawers and to change. In my business, I do not want managers to work from the office. I want them in the trenches with the rest of the crew, and I want to make sure management interacts with customers.

Of course, all of this is based on starting with a blank slate, a wall-free square box, but that is rarely the case when you rent or buy a building. You will oftentimes be forced to deal with preexisting conditions. For example, what is now Billy's already had a kitchen, but it was not the size I would have chosen had I started with a blank box. It is not where I would have put it, but the cost to gut the entire place—fixtures, gas, electric, the works—would have been prohibitive, so I worked with the hand I had been dealt. You may have to as well. These are the types of choices entrepreneurs face. Sometimes the answer is to start out conservatively and make alterations as you go. Maybe on day one you have to deal with a less-than-perfect design setup, but as you grow and hopefully thrive, you can do those major renovations that allow you to put everything exactly where you want. In a way, that is even more practical than simply renovating every few years just for the sake of cosmetic improvements.

Sometimes the limits of your design dictate your business model. Billy's has a kitchen so small I have to hire jockeys to cook for me. If I gain any weight, I'll get stuck in there and might never get out! In practical terms, this means we cannot do on-premises baking. I would love for us to bake our own stuff, but it simply cannot be done. See how design affects everything? If we ever somehow expanded and I could get a larger kitchen, I could add homemade baked goods, and Billy's would take on a whole new flavor—several new flavors, in fact!

The concept of design obviously has more intricacies such as employee area and rest rooms—which by law must be ADA compliant for handicapped people. The list of legal compliances is endless, so if you are a beginner, go to the city hall where your business will be located, tell them the type of business you're planning on opening, let them provide you with what their city codes require, and speak with the health department and other related departments and let them provide you with their information. Believe me, there are codes for everything—the size and design of your signage, the number of electrical outlets, fire suppression systems, on and on. It makes us all grumble, but the best and easiest way to deal with it is to go to city hall and ask questions *before* you do anything. It will save you a bundle. City hall is a pain in the you-know-what only if you don't consult it first. If you ask questions nicely, the people there will usually try to help. Remember, businesses are the lifeblood of a town. They provide jobs and they generate tax revenues. They want you there, they really do; you just have to follow the rules.

I recommend that you hire an architect. In some towns and states you cannot even get permits unless you have official architectural drawings for the town to keep on file. Depending on the size of the job, you can negotiate. In everything you do in starting your business, the key word is *negotiate*. It's up to you to make a bad deal, a good deal, a great deal, or no deal at all.

10

Facility Maintenance

Wow! You're on page forty-seven already. You're dedicated to making one of the most important decisions toward personal and financial freedom you will ever have the opportunity to experience.

In business, always be prepared for the element of surprise, and in my experience, nothing jumps up and takes us by surprise as often as facility maintenance. It's funny, but not really fun, as equipment usually breaks down on weekends or when you have an important meeting. It's Murphy's Law. I hate that law. On weekends and at night, repairmen charge a much higher rate. And then there's overtime, which will always creep up and bite you. Stuff happens, period. So what can we do?

- **Sign service agreements for equipment.** Cover your HVAC system, computers, and other large goods with service agreements. Be proactive in this matter; it's cheaper in the long run. Parts may also be hard to find. Service agreements may not prevent this from happening, but vendors tend to take better and faster care of their service agreement customers than their à la carte customers. Service agreement customers have made commitments to do business with them, so if you need a certain type of motor and so does some other guy who's just calling around, and they have only one in stock, it's more likely they'll give it to you and tell the other guy to wait.

  On this same subject, if certain parts of your business' vital equipment are more prone to breaking (think light bulbs), consider stocking them yourself. I know guys who literally have two machines just so they can scavenge one for spare parts for the other, but that's a little compulsive—and expensive. Still, a guy like that is probably never down, and being down can cost a lot more money than you might at first imagine.

- **Do regular maintenance on your equipment.** I guarantee that every piece of equipment you buy comes with an owner's manual. What do you do with it? Don't tell me you throw it away or I'll get mad. No; keep that thing on file, and keep them all together or else close by the equipment in question. And then (here comes the good part) *read them*! Yes, read the darn things. In most cases there will be suggestions on how to regularly maintain that piece of equipment. Most dumb slobs never read about that. Those are the guys who are always crying when their machine breaks right when they've got a big rush of business. If they had been following directions all along, oiling that machine every six months or whatever the booklet said, they might not be crying. Mark down in a calendar when to service your equipment. Then, like the sneaker commercial says, just do it!

- **Keep those doors of yours open.** When things do go awry, whatever you do, stay open. There's nothing worse than being closed. I'd rather make a tiny bit of money on a crappy day than make no money at all. Let's say your air conditioning crashes on the hottest day of the year. Some guys would close their doors and hang a sign that reads, "AC Broken—Go Somewhere Else." Me? I'd hang a sign saying, "AC Broken. All Meals 40% Off!" Then go out and grab all the fans you can and pray for the best. No, better still, instead of praying, *make it happen*! What I've just described for you is good old American ingenuity.

Customers will forgive you if you ask for forgiveness. Be honest with them and tell them your AC is busted, which gives them a choice, but then tip the choice in your favor by making them a deal, such as having a special sale that day. Keep your spirits light when they come in. Apologize for the high temperatures, but then sing or dance while you're carrying their plates—I'm only half kidding. If people see you're not upset, they won't get upset. As a business owner, you set the mood. They say, "Never let them see you sweat." Well, if you've got no AC, you'll have sweat pouring out of every inch of your body, but if you're wearing a smile, your customers will be wearing smiles too. A good attitude is infectious. I'll bet if you handle crises this way, not only will you make some money when things go badly, those customers will feel they've gone through an exciting experience with you. It's that feeling that we're all in it together, like we're all in the same foxhole or something. They'll come back a month later and say, "Hey Billy, remember that hot day when you had no air conditioning? Boy, I wish it was that warm today!"

- **Hire a landscaper.** Maintain the outside of your establishment, especially in winter months with ice and snow. You need to have your parking lots and sidewalks clean. Sweep up debris. If you don't, it will just collect, and people will drag it into your establishment. Some people are sue-happy, and others judge the outside appearance of a building as a reflection of the business inside. Franchises know this. Usually the first thing they do every few years is remodel the facade and landscaping, and this often increases business from fifteen to twenty percent. I hate to say it, but it's the cost of doing business.

I can only hope and pray you are so successful in your business that you hire folks to do all this. I used to hate shoveling snow and salting the walks in the winter. Thank God I don't have to do it anymore. But if I have to, I won't think twice about doing it myself to keep my customers safe and happy.

It is up to you to set the standards of your business. Set them high, and then exceed them. That's one of the secrets to your survival.

11

Getting the Bucks

As you can see, there are many hoops to jump through in building your business. You are probably asking when the madness will end. It doesn't. That is why it takes a special breed of person to do this. Furthermore, it takes a special breed of person to slog his or her way through books like this. Hey, reading is the price you have to pay to learn how to do things. But I promise I'll try to keep it light.

I love the term "financing," a fancy word for "begging." Look, it's not so bad. I promise you, you will get smarter with every deal. It will get smoother. It's always the first time your do anything that's usually the hardest. Think about the first girl or boy you asked out, your first day in school, your first time doing almost anything. What I will attempt to do in this chapter is build your confidence, but I need your help to do it.

The first thing you need to do is prepare before speaking to your bank or mortgage company in this manner:

- **Prepare a business plan**. Here is where your CPA comes into play. Speak to him about helping you create a business plan. Banks love it when businesses use the best accounting firms, because a good accounting firm adds weight to your proposal.
- **Check your credit report**. You do not want any surprises. Look for anything negative such as liens or derogatory remarks. You can dispute the items on your own. Equifax, TransUnion, and Experian, the big three credit reporting agencies, provide dispute forms on their Websites.

- **Know what to say and how to say it**. This is the next step after you know what's in your credit score and have a CPA and a business plan in place. You don't get a second chance to make a good first impression. You must be logical, knowledgeable, and passionate about what you are proposing. Practice a few mock interviews. You must be confidant. I believe people want to be sold, and your job is to sell yourself. If you can't do this, it's a bit of a problem, but you can fix it by bringing your CPA to the meeting.
- **Always ask for the maximum cash**. Like I said earlier about hiring professionals, it is better to have something and not need it than to need it and not have it. Most bankers will tell you why most businesses fail: *undercapitalization*. If you think you need $100,000, ask for $150,000. Believe me, you'll need it. I guarantee no matter how well you have written up your budget, what

you think you'll need before you open your doors has no relationship to what you'll discover you'll need once those doors are open. And as for estimating how much income you'll make in your first year—that's a fool's game. The truth is you have absolutely no idea, so imagine it will be tough going and you'll need to pull out all stops in order to get yourself started on your path to success.

Okay, let's look at some basic as well as some unorthodox ways of getting funds to do your business. Let me share with you what I did to buy Billy's Downtown Diner, which was dangerous and could have cost me my credit. Well, actually it did. It could also have cost the loss of my mom's home, which she had put up for collateral. I borrowed from family and friends, and I got an SBA loan at twelve percent (pretty darn high, but it could have been worse). Oh yeah, I forgot; my wife was pregnant with our firstborn, Panayioti, and I had quit a well-paying sales job. At the time I had finally come to realize there is a difference between a job and a career. Trust me, even if I had been making $150,000 a year—and I wasn't—to me, it was still just a job.

Here is what I did: I maxed out about twenty of my credit cards to the tune of $60,000, with interest rates ranging from twenty to twenty-nine percent. This was a dangerous move because I was using personal credit to pay for corporation debt. In business, we use corporations as a legal structure to protect our personal assets. I was throwing all that to the wind.

When I was buying Billy's, the building did not appraise well. We were purchasing the building at $312,000, and it appraised for $280,000. Damn, I was $40,000 short! This meant that using the value of the property as collateral would not cover the cost of buying the building. What did I do? I went to the one person who believed in me more than I believed in myself, and trust me, I believe in myself or I would not have even considered asking. I went to my mother. With a smile on her lips and a twinkle in her eye, she looked at my wife, Yanna, and me and without a second thought and knowing she could potentially lose her house, knowing that I had exhausted all my other options, she signed on the dotted line.

Why did we have to do this? Simple. Banks and other

lenders always want skin in the game—they want you to put your own money into your venture. This may come as a surprise to you, but a long, long time ago, a guy could walk into a bank with a great idea, and a banker would say, "Hey, that sounds good. How much money can we lend you?" Those days are long gone. Today, no matter how good your idea is, banks want collateral; they no longer offer unsecured loans. In other words, to borrow $100,000, you have to give them something worth about *$115,000*! They don't want something of the same value; they want some security that's worth at least fifteen percent more than the amount they are lending you.

Let me break it down even more. You're not actually giving them your house, you're giving them a *lien* against it; a promise that should something go wrong, it now belongs to them. Furthermore, you are giving them legal documentation that makes it easy for them to grab that thing of yours should you fail. I mean, they don't want you picking your house up in the middle of the night and taking it with you to Canada or something. Sometimes it's a house, sometimes it's a boat; it can also be stocks, bonds, what have you.

In addition to giving lenders collateral, they also want to see that you are putting some actual cash into your dream. They don't care where you got it; they just want to be sure they are not providing 100 percent of the financing of your business. It's no different from getting a home mortgage. In a perfect world, banks want to see you putting about twenty percent of your own money into a down payment, then they will be happy to lend you the rest in the form of a mortgage. In that way, if your house is valued at, say, $100,000, and you put up $20,000 of your own, the bank has a mortgage lien of $80,000, and if you go bust, they take your house, sell it at auction, and take their money out first. In that way, if the house has lost value and is worth only, say, $80,000, they get theirs, and you get nothing! That's why banks are rich and folks are poor. Bottom line: Lenders insist you put your own skin in the game. They want you to take the risk, not them.

Back to me… You want to talk about being nervous? I had the cold sweats. I could lose my credit, my mom could lose her house, and my wife and I could have potentially been homeless. All my wife and I had was each other, my mother, and a load of debt. I was scared; I'm not denying it, but I knew action cures fear. So my mom—then in her sixties—my wife, and I busted our asses. My mom was at the register; Yanna, whom I referred to as the "pregnant wife," acted as waitress (by that stage in her pregnancy she could often do little else); and I was the cook. Seven days a week we worked from 6 a.m. to 8 p.m. One goal, one vision, no excuses. No matter how sick any of us got, we would be there at the diner. My wife almost miscarried. Thank my dear lord Jesus Christ she didn't, and in two years the credit card debt vanished. We were able to remove the lien from my mother's house. (Thanks, Mom; I love you. You are my hero).

During our fourth year in business we won a readers' poll for best breakfast, and in our fifth and sixth years, best breakfast as well as best diner. Every time I think of how we did it, I cry like a little girl. Thanks to Mom, my wife, and God, we did okay.

Hey, the price of freedom does not come cheap. No risk, no reward. You must believe in yourself and work hard and smart.

Places to get financing

Credit cards lend money at a very high rate of interest. Better choices, if they are available to you, are commercial mortgage companies, the SBA (Small Business Administration), and home equity loans.

There are also private investors. You get, say, five people to each kick in some cash. I don't know how to structure that sort of arrangement, but your CPA or business lawyer does, so ask them about it. There are even Internet sites for people to lend each other money or to invest in business. One I know of is called angeldeals.com. Check them out.

Check if there are any Housing and Urban Development (HUD) loans available. They are usually available to restore or rehabilitate buildings and can often beat the interest rates of more-conventional loans.

Ask friends and family if they can lend you thousands. Or maybe you should just ask for hundreds. Seriously, never turn down any money; just don't sell your soul or make a deal with the devil.

The more realistic you are about your dream or business, the easier it will be to get financing. I've met hundreds of people who have said to me, "Billy, I wish I could open my own business just like you did, but I have no access to cash." The truth is where there is a will, there is a way. We all have access to cash; it's just a matter of how resourceful and how driven we are. If you quit before you start just because you weren't born with a silver spoon in your mouth and a million-dollar trust fund, you will always fail because you don't have the fire in the belly required to be an entrepreneur. Getting funding is just one of a thousand obstacles that are placed in your way. As they say, if it were easy, everyone would be doing it. It is *not* easy. Baby steps are a good way to start, and like a baby, they grow and blossom into something great.

12

Menu Creation (This Works Even for Non-Restaurants!)

If you have no desire to open a restaurant, you'll probably skip right over this chapter, which would be shame, 'cause I promise you it's a good one.

I have to relate everything to what I know: owning a diner. You? Maybe you're a snake charmer or a koala breeder; what do I know? I'll bet, though, you may have a hard time if you try to find a book on how to start your own snake-charming or koala-breeding business. But I have learned from meeting people from all walks of life that there are more similarities between successful businesses than there are differences. So all you snake and koala fans, keep reading.

When I opened Billy's, I had to ask myself, "How will my menu be different?" If you're a snake charmer, ask yourself the same question: "How will I be different from the millions of other snake charmers in the Lehigh Valley?"

The answer is *uniqueness.* No matter what your business is, it must be unique, or else why should it even exist? Mind you, you don't always have to be completely original and totally different to be better. Uniqueness is relative. It can be subtle, too. Look at McDonald's and Burger King. Everywhere in America, one is on one corner and the other is on the next corner. Are there differences between the two chains? Yes and no. No, because they both basically sell fast-food burgers and fries. Yes, because despite the hundreds of similarities, some people like one better than the other. Why? Because if you studied them hard, you would notice a few differences. Your own personal menu creation may be a lot like that too.

I own a diner. There are other diners around me. In Bethlehem, we have a lot of pizza parlors too. Check them out as well. Lots of similarities yet lots of differences too. Some don't sell slices. Some sell slices, but only the basics like plain, pepperoni, and sausage. Others sell all sorts of exotic toppings, including pineapple and ham, peanut butter and sauerkraut, and…okay, maybe not PB and kraut, but you get the picture. Is the classic place wrong for not keeping up with trendy new pizzas? Maybe, maybe not. Maybe they make the best darn pizza in the area, and why should they mess with success? Maybe the guy with the exotic pizzas is covering up for the fact his pizzas taste lousy; who knows?

Menu creation and concept are similar and yet different. As a diner, I can choose to have an ethnic, Greek concept, yet my menu creation is still up for discussion. There are all sorts of different Greek dishes. Some are very common, like gyros and pasticcio, while others are pretty exotic. In other words, you can go to twenty different Greek-themed diners, and each will have a slightly different menu. The same goes for whatever you do. Once you have your concept, the details are in exactly what services you want to offer. This takes careful study too. What services do your competitors offer? What are you good at?

Some people's businesses evolve over time in order to meet new needs. A lot of time that means adding more and more goods and services in order to create cash flow. I mean, sometimes I wonder about ice cream shops. They have lines down the block on a hot summer day, but who goes to those places in February? Some of them actually close for the season, some just gut it out, but others offer some other kind of product. The concept remains the same—it's an ice cream shop. But maybe you're the guy with an ice cream shop that also sells hot soup and hot beverages in the winter. That's your menu—literally. Maybe if you're in the eyeglass business, you sell fancy eyeglass chains as an accessory. If that takes off, maybe you add some handmade jewelry, since what is an eyeglass chain but jewelry anyway?

You have to create your menu to make maximum use of your space and make the maximum number of sales. Whatever it takes, you do it. Sometimes, instead of adding items, you may cut items. Why? Because of time, cost, and space! Maybe you added something to your menu, but hardly anyone is buying it. Meanwhile, you can't display more of some other item people want more of. You might also be wasting your time creating this other item or providing this other service, time you should be devoting to something else you do better or is a hotter seller.

I'll give you another restaurant example: brie cheese. It tastes good. You can put it in or on a lot of things. Lots of people like it. But it's expensive, and it doesn't last long. If you decide to put brie on your menu, you'd better be sure people will buy enough of it in a day or a week or else you will find yourself throwing out expensive brie that's gone bad and losing lots of money. Keep tabs on everything in your business. Profit is in the details.

A lot of this is trial and error. Businesses that last never rest on their laurels. They keep tabs on what's hot and what's not whether it's around the neighborhood or right inside their own four walls. You have to keep track of everything. If you just punch in and punch out every day, that's what I call "employee mentality." You're not an employee anymore—you're the boss! Think like a boss. Keep thinking. Just because the doors are open and money is coming in doesn't mean you can hang your brain out to dry. People who do that start to go downhill fast.

13

Pricing Your Services

Everybody has a price he or she is willing to pay for a product or service. As I said earlier, a fair price is what someone is willing to pay. When determining this, see what your competitors are charging. What are they giving? What is their reputation? Take your time. Be thorough. Do your research.

Let me lay it out in restaurant terms: in my business, customers want to know what they're getting, how quick will it take, and what it will cost. At the same time I need to know if I can give them what they want and still make a profit. I do it through a menu, a line-by-line inventory with mouthwatering descriptions to entice the guest to purchase the product. By the way, what I do is no different from slapping a great sticker price on an auto or a fancy designer name on a clothing label.

In developing my menu, I never exclude the customer's wants and needs. For example, I have spent more than half my life in restaurants and, believe it or not, I've never tasted Pennsylvania Dutch Treat Scrapple. Hell, I don't even know what's in it, but I can tell you one thing—we sell a boatload of it.

In pricing your services, don't bite off more than you can chew. In my diner, I know we kick ass with breakfast and lunch. I won't even consider introducing French cuisine. Well, maybe french fries! Seriously, I stick to what I know and what I'm good at. I know my competition, and I know my customers' needs and wants, and every day I am in my business dedicating all my time and energy to them. I listen to them. Some of the most brilliant menu ideas my wife and I got were from my customers. *Billy's Downtown Diner—Not Your Ordinary Cookbook,* my first book, is an autobiographical love story with our menus and recipes that is filled with some of our customers' ideas.

Sometimes you don't even have to look far to get

answers. Just look in the mirror. Be honest with yourself. Look for a niche. Be happy, and you'll be inspired. If you're feeling blue, let your pain and sorrow drive you to make a positive change in your life.

Pricing is a funny thing. It's often nothing more than perception. Take two restaurants (here I'm talking restaurants again, but hey, it's what I know best). They both serve a similar type of cuisine, but one sets its prices twenty-five percent higher than the other and also goes for a more upscale look. Suddenly, in the mind of the public, that place is the fancy place, while the other is the family place. The hilarity is that the food on the plate may be absolutely identical, yet people are willing to pay twenty-five percent more at one place because they *think* they're getting something *worth* twenty-five percent more! To this I say, hey, if you can get away with it, good for you. But if it doesn't work, don't be surprised. What's that line about fooling some of the people some of the time, yadda yadda?

Pricing is part of your concept. You can be the budget guy, the family guy, the discount guy, the fancy-schmancy guy, whatever. The only wrong answer is the one that doesn't work! But once you go for a certain pricing concept, you have to go all the way. You can't go high-end and then keep a slobby, rundown place. No customer is *that* stupid! You also have to believe in it and live it, day by day.

Another thing about pricing: you can't just set it and forget it. The economy keeps moving on, forever and ever, amen. Just because you shopped your competition and you looked at you inventory invoices when you opened does not mean you never have to do it again. Prices change. Maybe you charged thirty-five dollars an hour to fix computer printers when you first opened. Now it's four years later. You're still charging thirty-five dollars, but all your competitors are charging sixty dollars. What are you, a yutz? It would be one thing if you were advertising your low, low prices and people were coming to you in volume. But I know far more people who simply go to work each day with their heads down, unaware of what's going on in the world around them. As a business owner you can't do that. You have to know when the market has changed if only by a matter of pennies. It all adds up. That printer repairman who didn't know the market had gone up could have made nearly twice as much money on his service. That's money he'll never get back.

Last, though, you have to be ready to ditch your pricing concept and change directions literally overnight if you find you are tanking. I've seen guys start out high-end and shift to more-affordable prices. I've seen other guys start out as discounters and then shift to high-end. These are smart people who are always looking over their own books as well as checking out their competition. If your market gets flooded with too many clones and your business starts to drop, you'd better start brainstorming, and fast!

Don't refuse to leave a sinking ship. Entrepreneurs who never give up are the ones who last. Going down with the ship is a form of giving up because you're facing certain suicide but doing nothing about it. Instead, be the smart rat who jumps from the ship to a life raft and then onto another ship. Keep jumping, keep living, and you'll be a success.

14

Hiring Personnel

I don't know the business you're planning on getting into, but in my business I need people, and hiring and finding personnel is easy. Finding *great* personnel is a bitch, though; it's never an easy task. The first thing I highly recommend is speaking with an employment lawyer in order to get guidance. What you, as a novice, might think are perfectly innocent and acceptable questions to ask during an interview might actually get you sued. There are some serious lawsuits out there because of age discrimination, sex discrimination, religious discrimination, and many, many, others. You could find yourself on the wrong end of a lawsuit even though in your heart you haven't discriminated against anyone at all; you just said the wrong thing or asked the wrong question in the wrong way.

Here is a quick example: In Pennsylvania, you must be twenty-one to consume alcohol and eighteen to serve it. You can't ask your potential hires' ages, but you can ask them if they are over eighteen. See? It's all in the details. In business and law, you must choose your words wisely, and if you can't, hire someone who can.

A good way to start before conducting interviews is to purchase some standard job application forms. No sense reinventing the wheel. They are cheap, usually pretty standard, and can be purchased almost anywhere or downloaded off the Internet.

Make sure the potential new hire has filled out the entire application. Ask for references, and call all of them. It is important to know who you hire. Remember, the employees you hire represent you and your business. Always ask why they left their previous jobs, and let them know you are looking for a professional and not a job-hopper. Remember, a bad hire is a waste of your time and money and could potentially hinder the growth of your business. There is the old saying: better to be in no company than bad company.

Let me share a quick story with you. I was golfing for some fundraiser with Martin, my good friend and customer. We were on the ninth hole, and I was teeing up and getting into position to drive my golf ball 250 yards right down the center of the fairway. Okay, I'm lying; it went 100 yards hard right—no fault of my own, of course. It was because Martin's cell phone rang. Anyway, he answered it, and I heard him say, "Don't give Bob the job."

I was intrigued and had to ask, "Martin, times are tough. Why aren't you giving Bob a job?"

He took a sip of his beer and said, "Billy, he interviewed well; he had all the right answers."

So I asked again, "What's the problem?"

Martin said he always asked what he called the "deal maker or breaker" question when he interviews. His question was: "What do you do for a hobby?"

Bob had said that he loved golf.

Martin asked, "What do you shoot?"

Bob replied, "High sixties, low seventies," and then said he golfed three to four times a week.

I asked Martin, "What's the problem with that?"

He said, "Billy, in the interview, he expressed more passion about golf than why he wanted to work for me! Not to mention, if someone is that good at golf, that means that's his main focus. If he would have said he shot in the high eighties or nineties, chances are I would have hired him." Then Martin looked over at me and asked, "Billy if you shot in the sixties playing golf, what would happen to your business?"

I understood his logic and his great intuition. He said life is filled with priorities. If I would have focused on my hobby as opposed to my career, chances are I would probably have gone bankrupt.

15

Leadership Skills

The restaurant business is stressful. You need to be a multitasker. You need to know your products. You also need to know how to do every single job yourself because in the course of your business life you might have to do them all at one point or another. I mean, what do you think I do if the dishwasher calls in sick? I do the dishes! I wait tables. I work the register. Whatever has to get done, you have to know how to do it, and when the time comes, you have to do it. You can't close the doors and lose a day's income because Freddy is the only guy who knows how to do something and Freddy just called in with a hangover.

Your employees will ask you a thousand questions a day, everything from prices to schedules. The way you interact and communicate with them will either motivate them to work harder and smarter, or it will have the opposite effect. Frankly, I like it when they ask a question, and I hate it only when it's the same question I just answered. That's the balancing act. You don't want to be the boss who scares off questions, because when employees don't ask questions they simply do what they feel like doing instead of finding out how you, the boss, want things handled.

On the other hand, if I answer a question and then reinforce it by plastering it on a sign on the wall and someone comes back and asks me it again, I will know I've hired an idiot who has to be replaced. Don't keep people like that on your payroll. Employees are supposed to lighten your load, not make it worse.

Bad bosses rarely make it. The classic bad boss is the ogre who screams and yells at everybody, and the wimp boss who holds nobody to any standards at all is just as bad. The best boss is somewhere in between.

Understand your employees' needs

- You must be honest with your employees. Nobody likes his or her chain yanked. Be straight with people, and they are more likely to be straight with you.
- Don't be an elitist. This means lead by example. Nobody busts ass for bosses who think they're too good to get their own hands dirty. If your employees see you roll up your sleeves when it's needed, they will be ashamed to give you anything less than their own best efforts.
- Take the time to give honest compliments to your employees and to thank them for working for you. Small but sincere gestures like these can be great morale-boosters.
- Realize when they need help or are falling behind. Don't sit back and watch an employee fail, because *their* failure is *your* failure. Sometimes they

are just drowning in work and, for the sake of productivity, they need a hand. Crises can be teaching moments. Maybe they're falling behind because they're not doing things in the most efficient way. When this happens, they are going to be far more open to learning new and better ways to do things than when things are fine and you're just lecturing them.

Know your staff and their strengths and limitations

This is common sense. It's like basketball. You don't have the five-foot-eight guy guarding the seven-foot guy. He'll get killed every time. Business is the same way. You don't have the guy with zero math skills doing the books. He'll end up giving away all the money. And just like you can't yell at the five-foot-eight guy for being short, you can yell only so much at people when they fail at things they simply aren't wired to do well. The bad-math guy can be given a simple calculator or taught how to input numbers into a bookkeeping program since most programs like that do math for you these days. On the other hand, you can't ask the person who speaks no English whatsoever to be a waitress. It makes no sense. You can't learn an entire language by having pressure put on you. You have to understand all this right when you hire people; it's like casting a play. You get the right people with the right skills for the right jobs. If you do it right, then all you have to do is manage their attitudes, which you should *also* be screening for when you hire. Still, even the best people can develop bad attitudes if their boss has a bad attitude. If you hire good people and they underperform, maybe the problem is you.

Leadership is tough. You know that line "never let them see you sweat"? It's true. If employees see you panic all the time, they will panic all the time. If they see you always in control, they will do the same. If they see you with a smile on your face, getting along well with the customers, they will do that too. When you see bad behavior in your employees, right before blowing your stack ask yourself, "Do I do that too?" If so, take a good look in the mirror and see how you can improve your own performance. And then? Then don't just *tell* employees how to be better, *show* them how to do better by doing it that way yourself. People learn by example. As the boss, *you* are the example.

Leadership is the ability to get and give information. Your employees will rarely be asked to do research for your business. That's usually your job. It's also your primary job to watch what's going on, or at least ask the right questions. If you sit back waiting for employees to come to you on their own to tell you, "Hey boss, everybody's complaining about our prices," you may be waiting a heck of a long time. It's not their job because it's really not their problem. But as the boss, *everything* is your problem! Keep your eyes peeled. Ask questions. Ask your employees questions.

Giving information is another phrase for teaching. No matter how experienced your help, they need to be taught *your* way of doing things. Your way may be completely different from what they're used to. If so, whose job is it to make sure they do it your way? *Yours*! That goes to your ability to give information. If you're a bad teacher, they won't learn. Yes, sometimes you'll get an employee who is very slow on the uptake, but if you find everyone you've hired is slow on the uptake, maybe it's *you*! If so, work on. Heck, if it comes down to it, ask your employees why they don't understand where you're coming from. Their answers could be very enlightening. Maybe you're one of those guys who calls everything a "whatchamacallit." That can be very confusing. If you're that guy, learn the names of things. Also, let your employees know it's okay to ask you follow-up questions. Some bad bosses yell at employees when they ask questions, and so they stop asking. When they stop asking, they're also likely to start doing things all wrong. Then you'll *really* be PO'd!

Being a good leader also means being able to control a group. Yes, employees can smell blood, and if they find they can band together and bully you, you're dead. They have to always know that no matter how nice a guy you are, at the end of the day *you* are the boss, and even if every single one of them gangs up on you, your decisions are final.

Controlling a group also means realizing that at a place of business, everyone soon learns everyone else's business! It's hard to keep a secret. For that reason, understand that, for the sake of the entire group, you cannot confide in just one employee. Figure that whatever you say to one you've said to them all. Example: If Mary comes to you in tears, saying her dog died and she needs two days off, you can't say, "Well, okay, just promise not to tell the others." Ha ha ha! Within a month someone else will be in your office asking for time off for just as silly a reason, and if you say no, he or she will whine, "But you told Mary…" You control your group by controlling everything you say to each member of that group.

Being a boss means being disliked from time to time, so you have to learn to live with that. When making decisions, think through what's fair and what's right. Decide what is in the best interest of your business and do it. If someone doesn't like it, well, perhaps that's because all they're thinking about is themselves and *not* your business.

Casey Stengel, the great Yankees manager, said he had no trouble dealing with players one on one because all he thought about was what was best for the *team*. Not what was best for the one guy in front of him, but what was best for the team. Your business is your team. Do what's best for your business at all times, and you'll be a world champion.

16

Marketing Your Business

One of my favorite activities is finding ways to promote my business. The possibilities are endless. A lot of people think of marketing and promotion as a "one size fits all" kind of deal, but I've found that my best ideas spring from my business' concept. Let your concept take the lead when marketing and see what follows.

For example, because of my knowledge of the restaurant business, I do cooking demonstrations and teach cooking, I do small-business development, I have a radio show, and I've published a cookbook. See how it all flows from what I do? If you owned a gift shop, you would spin all your ideas off that. Think about it for just a minute and I'm sure you could come up with half a dozen ways to promote that sort of business, ways completely different from how you would promote a diner. Owning a business opens up doors of opportunities. You just have to keep your eyes open.

Of course, before getting into such niche things as cookbooks and cooking classes, there are the basics, the classics:

- **Signage:** How can you possible succeed if no one can see you even when they are driving right past? Find out the maximum-size sign your town allows and build it. Make it as big as the law allows. *Be seen!*
- **Flyers:** Pass them around. Again, check with your town so you don't get in trouble tacking them to trees or putting them on cars, but whatever is allowed, *do*! Celebrate your grand opening. Celebrate anniversaries. Heck, celebrate your *dog's* birthday, just find some kind of excuse to print something up. And what should you

put on your flier? A *coupon*! That's right. Just having your name and address on something means nothing. You have to give something away. Giveaways are a call to action. Give people ten percent off, give them a free soda, promise them a date with Angelina Jolie—I don't know, just give them a reason to hang onto that flier. Make the flier useful to the person holding it.

- **Samples:** Have your best-looking, most personable employee hand out samples of your signature item. It could be outside your business, it could be inside your business (even if they're already there, people *love* something for nothing), it could be at some open event like the town fireworks celebration or a chamber of commerce event. Just keep your eyes open for places and reasons to give out a free taste of your wares. People will remember.

- **Loyalty programs:** Offer something for free after a certain number of visits. Businesses are built on customer loyalty. You don't want to make just one sale with any person unless he or she is just passing through from Latvia. It is easier to get ten sales from one person who keeps on returning than to make one sale each to ten new people. Keep selling your existing clientele by giving them an incentive to come back. I know, a lot of people think, *Wow, marketing is expensive. It either costs to do it, or it means giving something away.* To that I say remember, the biggest expense is empty seats!

- **Customer comment cards:** These are another good idea. They're interactive and let your customers know you care about what they think. I've heard of businesspeople publicly posting comment cards that contained good ideas—once they cleared it with the customer who suggested it. That's further proof to anyone who sees it that yours is a business that listens to its customers.

- **Web presence:** Your Website doesn't have to be super-expensive, but in this day and age you've got to have one. People are moving further and further away from Yellow Page advertising, which used to be everyone's standby. Now, when people want to find, say, a saddle shop in Cheyenne, Wyoming, they probably check the Internet first, not the phone book, so be there!

17

Hiring a Manager

You're only human. You can't work every hour of every day, never take a day off, never have a vacation, and never get sick. Something's got to give. For that reason you have to have someone around who acts as your number two, your right hand, someone who can take on leadership responsibilities in case you need to step out to a meeting or something.

I am a firm believer in having a right-hand person. In my case I am blessed that I have my wife, Yanna, and a great crew. You need to have someone you can trust and can care for your place to maintain the integrity of what you do. Not to have such a person on hand is to not plan, and not planning is a bad thing.

Make sure you have an employee manual; every business needs one. It's your bible. It clarifies your expectations for the various positions in your organization no matter how big or small. Your manager needs to be able to follow and execute that manual. Without a manual, you constantly have to make things up as you go, which is inefficient. No, you will not be able to think of everything in advance, but there should still be guidelines. Also, if things are not written down, employees can always use that famous excuse: "I don't remember you ever saying that." If it's written down, case closed.

Of course it's not all about the manual, although that document is crucial. It is also about whom you entrust as your number two.

I look for managers who are:

1. **Responsible.** Managers have to be dependable and able to handle being the boss even if only for an hour or so at a time. They have to be you when you aren't there. That means they have to act like you and think like you. Your customers must not be able to sense

anything different when your manager is running the place and when you are running it.

2. **Experienced.** Management is something people work toward. No one starts out life as a manager. It is a position that is earned. On day one of your new business, you need someone with some experience. I like managers with at least five years' experience and with at least three years at the same place. This demonstrates two things to me: skill and stability. Once you have been in business a while, you can promote managers from within, but on day one, you can't turn to someone who is day one on his or her first job and just give him or her managerial responsibility. That's crazy.

3. **Hard working.** This goes without saying, although I said it anyway. A lazy manager is no help at all. Your manager should be the second-hardest working person on your payroll next to you.

4. **Able to open and close.** Your manager can't have severe work limitations. You don't want to hear, "I can't open, I have to get my kids off to school" or "I can't close, I have to take care of my elderly mom in the evenings." I sympathize with those sorts of situations, but my sympathies cannot imperil my business. My managers have to do whatever I need, whenever I need it. If they can't do that, if they have all sorts of limitations on when they can and cannot work, they're no use to me. Sorry.

5. **Knowledgeable about all positions.** Just as I, the owner, have to know how to do everything, so does my manager.

6. **Great ability to train.** As the owner, my job is to train the manager. The manager, then, needs to be able to train others if I'm not available to do that. If I can't teach, I won't last long in business. If my manager can't teach, he or she is not a good manager.

7. **Honest.** The more responsibility you give someone, the easier you make it for that particular person to rip you off. If you're handing him or her the keys, the alarm code, and the combination to your safe, you're in essence handing your life over to that person. What qualities do you demand from someone you give that much power to? The first is honesty. If you catch an employee in a lie, even a small one, he or she is *not* the person you ever want to make manager.

One last thing on employee honesty: employees are only as honest as they are given the opportunity to be. If you lay candy all over the place and take a week off from work, some of your candy will be eaten by the time you come back. No matter how honest people appear to be, you still cannot be foolish. Set a standard for your manager and your employees. Tell them, "If you want candy or anything else from me, just ask. If it's something reasonable, I will probably share it will you. But don't steal my candy; if you do, I will suspect you are stealing everything else too."

18

Customer Service

All entrepreneurs are in the customer service industry whether they want to admit it or not. Customer service is a unique blend of a love/hate kind of marriage. It is complicated common sense. Customer service is a mixture of give-and-take, negotiations, respect, profitability, and understanding. What makes this hard for most people is that they do not understand that words without actions or actions without words will usually not give them a favorable result. It is important to remember that bad customer service will result in fatal blows to your company. This is why most companies spend millions of dollars speaking about their service.

There are three top things that sell people on a company: *quality, price,* and *service.* In a perfect world you should have all three. But in our world sometimes you simply can't. If you're a small business, you probably won't be able to beat super-chain competitors on price. Your quality may only equal but not exceed theirs. That leaves one thing: service.

What do I mean by the give-and-take of service? Let's first hit the basics. You come to my diner, you order bacon, I bring you bacon. My job is to get the order right, get it to you quickly, smile, tell you a funny story, and make sure it's the best bacon I can muster. No cold bacon, no slab of uncooked, meatless fat, no long wait, no nasty snarls from me—just a couple of nice, crispy, tasty strips of bacon along with my buoyant personality. If I get any of this wrong, it's on me, and I had better fix it and fast.

What if I bring it to you and you say, "I didn't order this. I ordered sausage"? My job is to smile, tell you I'm sorry, and get you some sausage right quick. Now I know I got it right and you got it wrong, but you're the customer, and you don't want to hear that. I'm making a profit from you, and if I make you happy, you'll return, and over the course of your visits I will totally forget the bacon you turned away. Remember: the customer is always right even though the customer is *not* always right.

So what makes this complicated? There is a famous story about some lady who tried to return automobile tires to a famous clothing store. Clothing stores do not sell steel-belted radials! Nonetheless, this store, which prided itself on customer service, refunded her for the tires. *This is crazy*! The customer in this case was demanding too much of the store. I would not participate in any part of this because there's no upside to it. I would not want this person as my customer because this person is not really a customer! Customers enter into an arrangement with a service-giver. They agree to pay so many dollars for X and in return will receive Y. Simple. This is customer service. Giving money away to a totally unreasonable person will only encourage that person to demand more, and who wants that?

In my bacon example, what I've evaluated—and very quickly, I might add—is that I will not lose money giving this customer the equivalent of two sides for the price of one (I will probably have to toss her bacon—which sounds kinda kinky, but it's not). Even though I am right and she is wrong, I will lose in the long run only if I make a big deal out of it. The tire thing, though, is pure idiocy. That store made nothing and will likely never make any money from that customer.

Subtleties. A customer says the sausage is cold. I know it's not, but again, it's not worth arguing over. Fix the situation, smile, and move on. Give good service. What if the sausage *is* cold? Fix it, but at the same time change whatever is in your system that caused you to hand someone cold sausage in the first place. If some other customer walks in and says, "Gimme some free sausage, dammit!" ask them why. If they can't come up with anything that seems even a little logical, give 'em the boot and tell 'em to go try to get free sausage from the guy down the street! See? It's all complicated common sense. Customer service requires more on-the-spot thinking than anything else in business.

Remember the special times of the year. In most businesses, there are certain times when people are spending. If you're a florist, it's Valentine's Day. If you're a CPA, it's tax time. These are the fat times for you financially, but they are also the times when people are most apt to remember their experience with you.

For me, its things like Mother's Day. People like to take Mom out for brunch. They may come in to eat at my place a dozen times during the year, but if they're bringing Mom for Mother's Day, I better *bring it*! I better be at the top of my game. It is so easy for people to say, "Yeah, I call my CPA during the year, and he makes time for me. But during tax season, finding him is like finding Bigfoot. And when I do get him, he gives me ten seconds and he's blowing me off. I think I'll look for another guy." Those are the kinds of things people remember. Those are the things that drive customers away. I try my hardest 365 days a year, but on days like Mother's Day, I know the stakes are higher so the steaks have to be even better. (See what I did there?)

Customer service is about people. You can be a success in any line of work without being the best in the world at it. You can be the fourth- or fifth-best home contractor in your area and still make the most money and get the most jobs if you are good with people. People do business with people they like and trust. If customers like and trust you, you're golden.

Always think clearly. Always be fair. Always think long-term. Always remember that customer service is a bond, an agreement, a deal between you and the customer. It must be fair to both or else it's no good.

19

Stayin' Alive
(It Ain't Just a Bee Gees Song)

If you've made it this far, you've been reading for about an hour, and if you've taken all my advice, you've created a successful business in less than sixty minutes. Ain't life grand! And people have the nerve to say we live in a fast-paced world.

The trouble is, opening a business and sustaining it are two different things. Most businesses fail to survive more than five years. The reason for this is failure to follow all of what we've covered thus far. To open a business and last three or five years or so requires a firm foundation: proper capitalization, a good team, dedication to quality and service, etc. Without a foundation, your business collapses in a heap.

So what happens after three to five years? Why do some businesses last while others fall by the wayside? There is no one reason, but there are a few major ones:

ABE

ABE is not the first name of our sixteenth president. It is an acronym similar to ABC, which in the sales world stands for *Always Be Closing*. ABE is my dear departed father's favorite advice, along with "Don't do that in public!" ABE stands for *Always Be Evolving*. For an older guy, he was pretty evolved to have come up with that one, though I think maybe he just listened to a lot of Dylan (remember when he told us if we're not busy being born, the other option is dying?)

Another way Dad put it was in Greek, which would be Greek to most of you reading this, but loosely interpreted, he said, "Your eyes and your ears should steal." See what I mean by loosely interpreted? Stealing doesn't sound good, but what the saying means is that we must always be searching. We must always be taking note of things and learning new things. Only a fool goes through life with closed eyes and closed ears. It also makes crossing the street dangerous.

Many businesses die because they refuse to change. If you're in a technological field, this is pure insanity, but even something as seemingly consistent as food service must always be evolving. Today, almost every fast-food place has some form of Buffalo wings or Buffalo chicken, but it was only a few years ago that the only place you ever heard of such things was…Buffalo, NY. Maybe if you have a restaurant in historic Williamsburg that draws tourists wanting to try out George Washington's favorite meals, you can get away with not changing anything. But for the rest of us it's Darwinism: change or die. We have to change our menus, change our appearance, keep up with technology, market ourselves differently, etc. A business can never stand completely still. Businesses that let themselves go are like people who let themselves go. When some people reach fifty, they are fit, happy, healthy, and attractive. Others the same age look like they're at death's door.

Greed

We go into business to live the American dream and make a nice living. Fine. But some people go overboard and kill the golden goose.

A while back a buddy of mine told me about a restaurant he went to. The place didn't take reservations, and there was always a ninety-minute wait. Now, as a restaurateur, this is heaven. It's a license to print money. But word around town was it was constantly so crowded, no one—ironically—wanted to eat there anymore. Then the other day my friend said, "Billy, that place is going bankrupt! How can that be?"

My pal did a little investigating, and lo and behold he learned that the owners got so drunk on their own success they started living far above their means. Big waterfront mansion. Stable full of luxury cars. Couple of boats.

This is fine and good *if you can afford it.* They couldn't. They used their business like it was a charge card with no limit, except *everything* has its limit. Things eventually hit the fan, despite how successful their business was. They stood on the precipice of a choice: sell off their stuff to settle their debts, or reorganize and sell the business. They refused to give up their stuff, so they got rid of the business. They will likely still lose their stuff eventually because *stuff* doesn't make you money, your *business* does!

There are other ways greed can kill a business. In order to give yourself more, you cut your staff, you skimp on reinvesting in the business, and you let your equipment upgrades and maintenance go. It's one thing to do these things because you're truly broke and trying to hang on, but it's another when you're doing this to buy that new Mercedes. A real business owner ditches the Mercedes for a Ford and keeps his or her business thriving. Again, stuff doesn't make you money, your business does.

Assets and liabilities

Your business is your greatest asset. Treat it that way. Your things—your home, your car, your boat—are liabilities. Don't invest in liabilities. Invest in assets. Once you've invested in your business, you will have to reinvest in it over and over again. If you don't, it will turn to crap, and you'll suddenly find yourself with no clients and no cash flow.

Boredom

Call it boredom, call it sloth—what I'm talking about is when a business simply stops caring. You used to go to a restaurant that served the best veal around. But veal must be high quality, and it must be pounded thin and tender. Have you ever gone to a place that once served great veal, then went back a year later and the meat was tough and rubbery? That's a sign of not caring.

Service

The first thing to go in most businesses is service. The stock on the shelves remains pretty much the same, but the staff no longer seems to care. Why? Because the boss no longer seems to care. If the boss is always out on his boat fishing or if he can't be bothered making the customers happy, why the heck should his staff care? Bosses need to remain hands-on. They have to love their business and act like every day is their first day.

Easiest way to check whether the boss still cares? Cleanliness. If the boss bends down to pick up a piece of trash, so will the staff. If he or she doesn't, nobody does. A business on its way out is messy and dirty. Cleanliness is a part of your service to the public.

Why does this happen? Bosses become jaded. Their business becomes just another job to them. They're bored. They're happy with the income they're getting, so they've closed their eyes and ears to ways to make it grow. They lose the hunger. The problem is, when you say to yourself, "I make $X, and that's enough," you're actually not going to remain at $X. That's the folly. You can't stand still in the middle of the ocean. Tides will always be going in and out, and currents are always pushing you one way or another. Try standing still, and life will toss you up against the rocks. Standing still actually takes a lot more effort than people realize. *Really* standing still takes a lot of work. Most guys who decide to stand still are really telling fate to take them and throw them against the rocks, which hurts like hell.

I have cameras at Billy's. I watch my staff even when I'm not there. I was at a Yankees game a while ago, and from my iPhone I noticed a napkin lying on the floor. I called the restaurant and asked, "Is somebody going to pick that up?" I'm like Big Brother, and I don't mind who knows it. Even when I should be out having a good time with baseball, Cracker Jack, and beer, I'm still thinking about Billy's. I watch the staff when I'm there but in another part of the restaurant. If someone is scratching his or her butt while walking down the aisle in front of customers, I take a cell phone picture of it. I don't do this to ream people out. In cases such as I just described, I actually make my employees laugh at themselves. The underlying message, though, is clear: You don't do that. That's unprofessional. Rearrange yourself in the bathroom and make it snappy. Bosses who are bored don't bother doing things like this. They're too busy with other things, like fishing and golfing. Me, I'm busy with Billy's, and I like it that way. I like it enough to keep my employees on their toes.

Remember how I described my first day ever at Billy's? If you forget, go back to the beginning of the book; I'll wait. I still feel the same way I did that first day every day. I get in first thing in the early morning and I stare at the door. I anxiously get the place in order, ready for my first customer, and I'm excited. I know it probably sounds crazy after all this time, but I love what I do. My business is not merely a means to an end. I do it because not only does it feed my family, but it also makes me happy. I'm living my dream. If you're not living your dream, take some time to figure out what that dream is and then do it, because if it's not your business, the business you're in right now, your business will fail.

If you want to get out of your business and into something else, sell high. Yeah, I know, it's old advice, but it's still true. If you wait until you've become bored and you've let the place slip, you'll get a lousy selling price if any at all. Sell when you're at your peak. Sell when people are *asking* you to sell because your business looks so darn lucrative. Then take the money and do something else that makes your soul sing.

People can spend their money anywhere. When you consider that, humility should wash over you. Why me, Lord? Why do people wake up and come to my little place for breakfast? You have to maintain that level of humility and thanks for every single customer. You can never take any of it for granted. The moment you do, someone young and hungry will come along and steal your clientele.

New business

My dad always said, "The kiss of death in a business is when all your customers are regulars." I told you my dad was a genius.

Older businesses can get like this. They have the same crew of customers day in and day out. It makes you happy as a businessperson; it makes you comfortable. It should also make you nervous. He who is not busy being born is busy dying. If all your customers are regulars, you aren't bringing in any new customers. Go find some! You're in trouble, but you don't even know it. Just because your books are balancing doesn't mean things are good. Know you're sick before you suddenly drop dead. Try something, do something, figure it out.

Stayin' alive is what it's all about. Success is measured by volume and longevity. I mention longevity because you can't look at life like some young pro athletes do. Some of those guys seem to have no idea that the millions they make annually will be earned for only a handful of years, and then that money has to last them the rest of their lives. Instead, they make a ton but spend that ton living large, and then it's onto the bread line. Businesspeople can make the same mistake. They hit it big, make a lot of money, and then they expect it all to sustain forever on its own. When it doesn't, I've seen guys who had been running their own businesses and driving new BMWs later hanging their heads out of drive-through windows and asking, "You want fries with that?"

Keep working. Keep thinking. Plan for your future. Spend less than you make. If you want to retire early, make sure you have enough to live on at the level to which you are accustomed. But bear in mind, none of this happens by accident. You have to make it happen. Businesses don't open by themselves, nor do they stay open by themselves.

America gives you opportunities no other country in the world can offer. The shame is in choosing to think it's all for the other guy and not for you. I'm no genius (my wife will vouch for that), but if I can make it, you can make it. It just takes an idea and dedication.

All the best to you and your dreams!

Please visit us at www.billysdiner.com

Also by Billy Kounoupis:
Billy's Downtown Diner: Not Your Ordinary Cookbook

10 E. BROAD ST.
Beth

610 867-0105